from Laurie and Dick
Christmas. 1969

Stillmeadow Album

STILLMEADOW ALBUM

ALBUM

by Gladys Taber

Photographs by Jacques Chepard

———— ❦ ————

J. B. Lippincott Company

Philadelphia and New York

Books by Gladys Taber

Stillmeadow Album (Photographs by Jacques Chepard)

Especially Dogs—Especially at Stillmeadow

Stillmeadow Calendar

One Dozen and One

Gladys Taber's Stillmeadow Cook Book

Another Path

The Stillmeadow Road

Stillmeadow Sampler

Stillmeadow Day Book

Foreword

Gladys Taber and Stillmeadow need no introduction, but since *Stillmeadow Album* is a unique venture, a few words to explain how it came about may not be superfluous.

The place called Stillmeadow is already dear and familiar to the readers of Gladys Taber's books and columns, and when a place is loved it's natural for people to want to *see* it, to *be* there. Jacques Chepard began to photograph Stillmeadow some years ago (a few pictures in the *Album* were used to illustrate Mrs. Taber's column "Butternut Wisdom" in *Family Circle*), and when the idea developed for a book combining text and pictures he returned again and again to capture its beauty, peace and lovableness in every season of the year.

The happy conjunction of these photographs and the text by Gladys Taber herself provides the next best thing to really *being* there.

T. H.
J. B. Lippincott Company

The country road dips down the hill to Stillmeadow past Jeremy Swamp and the old apple orchard. Old stone fences mark both sides and giant sugar maples arch over it.

The small white salt-box farmhouse stands behind the picket fence with the wrought-iron cocker-spaniel sign welcoming friends. The cocker is especially appropriate because at one time there were thirty-five cockers racing around the yard, plus two Irish setters, three cats and three small children. We raised and showed the cockers and trained them and the Irish for obedience as well as the show ring. The children loved the country living.

In January snow drifts along the fence. In June the Silver Moon climbing rose opens beside the gate, and summer walks down the path past the old well house.

"*T*urn right at the mailboxes," we tell friends who come from far away. The mailboxes are a welcome landmark on Jeremy Swamp Road, and two of them belong to Stillmeadow and our only neighbors who live beyond us up the hill. The narrow road leads to Kettletown, but is almost impassable beyond the two houses.

Kettletown, bought from the Indians for a kettle, has long since vanished, except for one or two ancient gravestones hidden in the thickets.

The other six mailboxes belong to neighbors along Jeremy Swamp Road, and the mail carrier leans out from his sturdy car to fill them as he goes on his daily round. Sometimes he ties packages to them around the holidays, and sometimes he leaves a note saying, "6 cents postage due."

My granddaughters, nine and seven, find going for the mail exciting. As they walk up the road they see an occasional fox, or the ruffed grouse that lives by the swamp, or a woodchuck. It's much more exciting than opening a mailbox in the city!

*T*his is the first view of Stillmeadow as you come up the country road, and it is one of my favorites, since it shows the early salt-box construction with the big central chimney and the original front door, which nobody ever uses.

Stillmeadow Champion Hollyberry Red wants to give a warm Irish welcome to the next guests and has already heard the sound of a car on Jeremy Swamp Road. Holly, I always said, would welcome a burglar with open paws. But an old dog breeder said, "Never underestimate your Irish. Just let someone frighten you and you'd see what happened."

The very early houses in Connecticut were usually salt-box, built around a central chimney. The steep roof encouraged the heavy snows to slide down harmlessly. There was at one time an extra tax on two-story houses, and the salt-box such as Stillmeadow could be listed as a one-story house since front and back were one story. However, three bedrooms and two closets were tucked in under the peak of the roof! The closets became bathrooms in the modern era. (Closets are important, but bathrooms more so.)

The hand-cut shingles catch the sunlight and cast lovely uneven shadow lines. The windows have the early twelve-over-eight small panes, and some still have bubbly glass in them.

The woodpile is stacked near the back door, reaching up to the windowsill. The wood comes off our own land from dead or storm-torn apple and maple trees.

$\mathcal{T}$he door from the back kitchen leads to the path to the pond. The back kitchen and woodshed were added sometime in the 1700s, for the original hand-cut shingles are still under one wall of this addition. The woodshed in those early days provide the nearest thing to a bathroom the house afforded.

The white brick barbecue by the pond was built by Smiley Burnette when he came to visit from Hollywood. He spent most of the time he was at Stillmeadow laying the bricks and setting in the grill. He was a big gentle man, with warmth and wisdom, and a determination never to eat a meal indoors! Before he and his lovely wife, Dallas, flew back to the world of movie-making, we christened the barbecue with a steak he cooked and served with his special sauce. We have always called it Smiley's barbecue.

$\mathcal{W}$hen the wisteria is in bloom, the old well house is almost hidden. In spring the song sparrows nest on top of the beams and fly in and out all day carrying twigs to make the nursery a snug place.

The well was dug by hand by the builder of the house and lined with hand-hewn boulders. A windlass and chain once held the bucket which was lowered to the cool shadowed water. Now the water is piped into the house and unromantically pumped by electricity. But you can still lift the cover and look down to the mysterious depths, and smell the dark sweet smell of the spring water.

Our plumber was doing this one day and his glasses fell from his pocket, and they are still at the bottom of the well!

*J*une afternoons are tender and luminous. The grass is dewy, velvet-soft, and the shadows of the giant sugar maples fall gently on the ancient farmhouse. The back door is hidden by the white lilac bush, and the wisteria reaches to the roof of the well house.

This back view of Stillmeadow shows the small roof of the borning room. This room was always built just off the keeping room (which was kitchen, dining room, living room). Some heat from the great fireplace in the keeping room helped keep the mother and newborn baby warm.

Inside the house now in daytime, the light is green and shadowy, for the maple shade makes a thick canopy.

*T*wo brooks tumble down the hill past the apple orchard and pour their water into the pond. At the lower end the water falls over the stones and flows past George's barn.

Indians camped here in the early days, and bits of pottery and arrow points are still around. Later a cabin stood at the edge, and the summerhouse is built on that ancient stone foundation. Perhaps the first family lived in the cabin while the men were struggling to hew the great timbers for the farmhouse.

The pond is a haven for wild ducks and muskrats and fish—including rainbow trout from the state hatchery. It is also just right on hot summer days for two small girls who love to swim.

*T*he summerhouse is cool and inviting in July and August, but in very early spring it has a special charm. The surface of the pond reflects the pattern of budding branches as the sun walks down the sky. The roof of George's barn is visible now, although later the foliage will conceal it. One light from the kitchen shines as dusk deepens. The mysterious, wistful sound of the peepers brings the essence of spring.

At suppertime whoever is cooking rings the bronze cowbell, and the family gathers for baked pork chops and cabbage or Stillmeadow beef stew.

In summer my son-in-law uses the summerhouse for his own writing and enjoys the quiet coolness. Late in the afternoon, when he is through for the day, guests and family gather there for snacks and iced drinks.

*O*riginally there were four apple orchards on the farm, but only a few trees are left, just enough to fill the air with the sweetness of apple blossoms in spring.

The road is too narrow for cars to pass, but there is almost no traffic, since the road to Stillmeadow just wanders up the hill to the woods. In winter one neighbor rides by in a sleigh drawn by a steady white horse. George, who owns the barn across the road, drives his truck over to the barn twice a day when he comes to feed his steers. But traffic is scarce, and the sound of a car usually means company has come to sit by the open fire and have tea.

George's barn stands with the dignity of time itself. It is across the road from the pond with the brook running by the end. The color is that faded red which old barns should be, if they are painted at all.

This was farm country, although the rocky soil of New England made farming grueling work. Most of the farmers gave up and went to work in factories in other parts of the country. George himself no longer lives in the house across the road, but he still raises black steers, which occupy his barn. Sometimes they get out and wander over to the pond to crop the sweet wild grass, and someone runs to the phone.

"George, they are out!"

I always hope he doesn't come too soon, for I think the patient animals love the taste of freedom.

*T*he hill above the pond slopes toward an apple orchard, and daffodils and narcissuses make a carpet of gold and white when they open in the sun-sweet spring air. Wild dark violets grow there too, and this is where my unicorn comes in the moonlight in May.

The first bulbs were planted a long time ago by Jill, the gardener of the family. Her method of planting was to take a basket of bulbs and toss them on the slope and then plant them wherever they fell. This gave a natural look when they first bloomed, and now they have spread and multiplied as they wished.

In the moonlight it looks as if handfuls of stars had fallen from the sky.

Under the trees at the top of the hill, morels grow, those delectable mushrooms shaped like Christmas trees. We slice them lengthwise and broil them in butter, and we like them better than truffles.

*C*loud patterns in May promise a thunderstorm to come. Above the bright green and blossoming earth, there is suddenly a new ceiling which darkens gradually. Then the thunder rolls on over the hills, and lightning flashes, and the quick rain comes down.

A thunderstorm, my father said, shows the magnificence of nature. He used to go out and stand in one just to admire the lightning. I prefer to sit quietly indoors and trust in God and the lightning rods and the copper cables on the giant maples around the house.

After the rain there will be a fresh crop of asparagus.

$\mathcal{T}$he Franklin stove stands on the hearth in my bedroom and study.

The first thing we did when we came to Stillmeadow was to open up my bedroom fireplace. That night it turned cold and Jill started the furnace. Smoke and soot simply poured from the opening in my room, so we discovered the hard way that the reason this one fireplace was closed was to make a flue possible for the furnace! But when the man came to close the opening, he told us we could still have a small stovepipe going into the flue.

The hunt for the Franklin stove ended in a junk shop where we rummaged for bits and pieces. Just as we were leaving with various rusty bits of iron, I kicked a pile of burlap, and underneath lay the elegant top of the stove. The design was beautiful under the dirt of years. If you lift the top you can put a kettle on the stove plates underneath and have tea by the glow of the fire.

The modern desk seems out of place in a 1690 bedroom. But next to it the antique maple daybed fits under the small-paned windows, and the Franklin stove and maple four-poster do belong.

Faith Baldwin and Keats lend inspiration, and cockers and Irish watch from the wall. A special water color from Ted Key hangs under the lamp, with Hazel holding an armful of dogs.

From the windows the view of the meadow is always lovely, whatever the season. And the road to Jeremy Swamp can be seen.

The room is a gathering place for the family and friends, perhaps because it once was the parlor. One front door opens from the entry next to it, but this is known as the dog door, since only the dogs have used it. People come in the back door according to Connecticut custom.

Usually when I work there is an Abyssinian kitten helping hit the typewriter keys with delicate seal-brown paws or chasing the carriage.

*T*he front room or parlor is used only on rare occasions because the fireplace is smaller than the great one in the keeping room, but it is a sunny pleasant room with plenty of shelves for books and records. Actually the only rooms at Stillmeadow without bookshelves are the upstairs bathroom and the downstairs shower.

The wallpaper is the old Whistler pattern in soft cranberry and green, and the big braided rug repeats these colors. The Chippendale chair was my grandmother's and has no value because at one time someone cut off a few inches of the legs. I have no idea why!

The hinges on the Dutch door are hand-wrought iron, and the door handles have the lovely heart shape.

The Christmas tree belongs in this room, and traditionally the presents are opened here, with the whole floor adrift with colored papers and ribbons.

The small front room was once called the parlor, but we call it simply the front room. Perhaps the word "parlor" suggests a Victorian elegance this simple pine and maple room does not have. The braided rug and soft cherry and green Whistler wallpaper give it a serenity that visitors enjoy.

One wall is covered with bookshelves to the ceiling, and there are more books and treasures in the open-door cupboards. There are two of these cupboards, and I often wonder whether they originally had the batten doors, but there is no sign of hinges or latchware.

The milk-glass pairs of lamps on the mantel bring back many memories of sunfilled October days hunting for just one more—just one more to match! These have the unbroken chimneys, so this mantle is one place the Abyssinian kitten is not welcome.

The clock was made in Connecticut in the early days and winds with a big iron key. It strikes the hours with a melancholy sweetness.

This is the Christmas room, for the tree stands by the hearth and the gay parcels fill the twin sofas.

*T*his built-in cupboard in the parlor houses a set of dark green goblets found in a captain's house in Maine. A matching cupboard is beside the fireplace. The wide-batten door to the keeping room has the original hand-wrought heart handle.

You can see through this door a bit of the keeping room itself, and beyond that the kitchen which has a plate rack over the range full of cypressware plates. The cypressware is a purple-brown design on a pale background.

Sunlight falls on the wide oak floor boards and the parlor hearth with the wide hand-hewn hearthstones. The floor boards all over the house are hand-cut boards pegged with hand-made square-headed nails. I always wonder who first decided to make nailheads round instead of square.

$\mathcal{T}$he trestle table and benches stand under the windows in the keeping room. They were an adventure in carpentry by Jill, my lifelong friend and mainstay of Stillmeadow. The solid maple top and hand-pegged construction make them look antique, and indeed thirty-odd years of constant use have given them the patina of time.

Family meals are served at this table, Scrabble is played on it and the grandchildren, nine and seven, find it a good place to make valentines or cut out paper dolls.

The milk glass is a part of the milk-glass collection, and the decorated enamel coffeepot came down in the family.

When we sit down to supper we say grace at this table, asking God's blessing on the world.

The old corner cupboard with the H hinges was in the house when we came. The milk-glass collection began with the blackberry spooners and just kept growing. There is a memory attached to every piece, from the swan compote found under a pile of old rugs in a junk shop to the covered dish with the hand on top and a green jewel on one finger, which came from a country auction.

The early milk-glass makers, I am told, used a type of sand in the process which modern glass makers do not have. In any case, once you collect a few pieces, you would never confuse the authentic pieces with the modern copies, although the patterns are copied. The modern piece is opaque with a glassy surface. The old piece has an opalescent glow and a soft sheen.

Finally, if there is any doubt in my mind, I pick the piece up and feel it carefully, especially along the design and edges. I cannot analyze the difference in feeling exactly except to say that in the old there is a softness, almost a fragility. The best way for anyone who wants to collect this loveliest of glass is to take a fully authenticated piece in one hand and a modern copy in the other, and look at them and feel them.

$\mathcal{W}$ith milk glass it is hard to choose a favorite pattern. It is usually the one you are looking at. The hand-and-dove covered dish is one I love. This is an oblong dish with lacy edge and on the cover is a delicate hand holding a dove (I have no idea why). A jeweled ring is on one finger. On some the jewel is missing, but the green glass emerald is on mine.

The blackberry spooners are the result of much hunting, as is the blackberry cream pitcher. The swan pattern is one of the most graceful, and the swan compote is especially dear to me because it slants on the base, showing some glassmaker was dreamy the day he turned the base. The swan salts are lovely with spring wildflowers in them.

I believe in using a collection, and we do use the milk glass, but I am careful to wash it in warm, not hot, gentle soapsuds and dry it with a soft towel. The lacy-edged vegetable dishes are used for fruit or flowers, but not for very hot vegetables.

*T*he heart of Stillmeadow is the great central fireplace in the keeping room. In the afternoon, sun falls on the hearth from the windows in the opposite wall. At dusk the fire sends an apricot glow over the narrow room. The original iron crane is handy for hanging the soup kettle over an applewood blaze. The grandchildren toast marshmallows here and the grown-ups pop corn.

The milking stool is a comfortable seat on cold winter nights, especially when Holly, the Irish setter, takes up the entire small sofa on the opposite side of the hearth.

Originally all of the cooking was done at this fireplace, and the oven at the back is big enough to roast a pig. The oven would be heated by raking in coals and pushing a wooden cover over the door. At the right time the cover was taken off and the coals raked out. Then the bread or roasts or hams were put in and the cover replaced. The hand-made bricks lining the oven retained enough heat to do the cooking, and on Thanksgiving Day the crisp juicy turkey was lifted out with wooden paddles.

When she was smaller, Anne, the younger grandchild, enjoyed tumbling around on the wide oak floor in the keeping room. Since 1690 countless children must have crawled on this same floor and taken their first wavering steps across it.

Anne is a cheerful, sturdy child who loves the world and advances to meet every new experience. I think she will aways have the capacity to enjoy everything to the utmost and to welcome whatever life offers.

The cycle begins again in the ancient farmhouse as a young voice rings out and wondering dark eyes look toward the sunlit window.

*H*olly, the champion Irish setter, shares her sofa with a dreamy small Anne. Both of them look with interest at the little black box that makes flashes of light as the picture is taken. A camera is a constant surprise.

Holly, from the time she was eight weeks old, loved small children. She bore patiently with one who wanted her to wear spring flowers in her collar, or have a valentine tied to her identification tag. She chased balls (which bored her) just to please an eager youngster, and she was generous with one who got down on the floor and ate out of her own feeding dish with her.

It was a very short time after this picture was taken that Anne was running across the floor to kiss Holly good night and to hug her in the morning. The love was fully shared, for Holly always gave Anne a warm kiss back and waved her elegant plumed tail happily.

Children and dogs and cats have always belonged together at Stillmeadow.

$\mathcal{H}$olly looks doubtful as company comes, for she knows somebody may have to have half of her sofa instead of standing against the wall all afternoon. Most guests pull up straight chairs and say, "Oh, don't disturb Holly. That is her own couch."

Occasionally a stranger may comment that dogs belong on the floor, but we never pay any attention. During March, the month of mud, we put India prints over the upholstered furniture and do not shoo dogs, cats or children off. India prints wash well and are inexpensive.

I believe a house is for those who live in it, rather than being something to live up to.

When she is not on the sofa, Holly prefers the warm hearth, especially on a bitter winter day. Like all very old houses Stillmeadow is drafty, and the open fire is exactly right for basking.

The hearthstones are wide and long, and there is plenty of room for the Irish to stretch out and relax. After a wild plunge in the snowdrifts, she waits to be toweled thoroughly, until her mahogany coat shines like satin. Then she gives a happy sigh and lies down to toast herself.

From the earliest days in history, when men learned to start a fire by rubbing sticks together or beating two stones against each other to strike sparks, an open fire has been a symbol of comfort. Mankind made an early alliance with dogs, who could help track game and bring it in. As a reward the dogs got a few bones and a chance to lie by the fire.

Holly does not have to help bring in food in order to occupy the hearth. She assumes, quite rightly, that it belongs to her.

*E*specially Me, commonly called Teddy, was the lord of the manor. When he was an elderly gentleman, he lost his hearing, but this did not affect his behavior, since he was obedience-trained and could follow any hand signals.

Occasionally, when a good many cars were driving up, Teddy and Kon-Tiki were put in the kennel run, ordinarily reserved for bitches in season. Otherwise the kennel house was seldom used, although the electric heat was cozy and the rest of the building a playroom for the children.

At Stillmeadow we once had thirty-five cockers, two Irish setters and three cats, but all of them were house residents.

Teddy was patient until the cars drove away and he could safely come out of the run without danger of being killed by an auto. As for Tiki, he went in to keep Teddy company, of course!

The main area around the house was fenced in after seven or eight cocker puppies and an eight-week-old Irish setter decided one day to go up in the old apple orchard and explore. It took the whole family quite a long time to catch them all.

The fence was a great help except when strangers came through the picket gate and left it open. No matter how busy the cockers and Irish were, they had a sixth sense about the gate being open and simply flew to dash out and down the road.

So we spent some time deciding on the wording of a sign, which we finally painted. I felt "Beware the Dog" would not be fair to our dogs because they loved everybody. "Watch Out—Dogs" also implied something I did not like.

We finally solved it with a simple request not to let the dogs out. We also put a table by the sign where visitors could drop packages while they opened and *closed* the gate. This was a board top fastened to the base of an antique sewing machine with a nice wrought-iron design.

*T*iki, Holly, Teddy, and Linda are the welcoming committee on this snowy day as guests arrived.

If the guests do not want snowy paws planted on their coats and wagging tails making snow flurries in the air, they must wait outside the gate until the cockers and Irish are persuaded to go back in the house and get dried off with warm bath towels. Then the visitors can tiptoe in.

Most guests who come to Stillmeadow are true dog people, however, and an ecstatic meeting begins the minute the picket gate is opened.

Jill

The Quiet Garden is a small fenced-in area at one side of the yard behind the house. It was a trash heap and wild-blackberry tangle when we came to Stillmeadow. A few flagstones were under the debris, showing there once was a small building there—perhaps a milk house.

The border of the garden was planned to be all white, but eventually a few pink hyacinths came in as well as a Peace rose. Lilies of the valley overflowed one corner, and narcissuses and Nicotiana send their delightful fragrances through the air in season. Sedum and white violets grow between the stones.

On a summer afternoon iced mint tea is served in the Quiet Garden while the sun lingers above the treetops and the air is dreamy.

*T*he woodpile is the countryman's treasure. On bitter winter nights, the open fires send a cozy warmth into the rooms, and at Stillmeadow the hearth is the heart of the home.

The dear neighbor who cuts the wood builds the woodpile entirely from what he cuts on his land and ours, and no living tree is ever cut. Dead trees are carefully felled and sawed up and seasoned and stacked near the back door. In summer, the woodpile may be up to the windowsills of the keeping room, but by spring, it will be only three or four feet high.

My favorite firewood is apple, for nothing smells quite like an applewood fire, but most of the dead apple trees have already gone. The sugar maples suffer from storm damage in winter and lose limbs as thick as a small tree. The elm-tree blight meant the elms had to come down, a great tragedy. Yet it is comforting to think that they do not rot away in a dump but give a comforting warmth on snowy nights.

*T*he world is big and mysterious when you are very small, as Anne was when she adventured all by herself into the back yard wanting to play with the cockers and Irish. When she found they were busy digging where the skunks lived, under the storage house, she tiptoed back to the house and had a little difficulty negotiating the old stone steps to the back kitchen.

For some reason this is a narrow door, although it is the most used of any of the five doors. This is the door the wood must come through, and it is a trick to get the big logs in. It is also the door nearest the Quiet Garden, the back yard, the gate to the pond and the grandchildren's swing and slide.

The stone steps are hand-hewn and a bit high for Anne, but Anne never gives in. There will, I think, never be steps in life that she will not try to climb!

$\mathcal{L}$ooking across the pond from the old apple orchard, the corner of the screened summerhouse is visible, and beyond it at the very edge of the swamp one of the two buildings we call the pheasant houses. They were built by the preceding owner, who planned to raise pedigreed pheasants. Nothing much came of this because he murdered his wife and killed himself one moonlit midnight.

The pheasant houses have played varied roles. They have been storage houses, kennel units for female cockers in heat, summerhouses. One of them currently is a play place for the two granddaughters, where they can paint and spread out their toys on rainy days and cut paper dolls and not have to pick anything up when company comes!

*T*he stairs in the houses of 1690 were ladder-steep. Those gracious curving stairways in Georgian houses imply a different and elegant era. At Stillmeadow the stairs are so narrow that behind the stair-well door is an outside door called the coffin door. This enabled the coffin-bearers to get the casket down from the upper bedrooms and out of doors.

We installed a ship's rope from Provincetown on Cape Cod as a handrail for people trying to negotiate the stairs safely.

The borning room opens off the stairway, with the keeping room and great fireplace near enough to provide some warmth. There is no fireplace in the borning room.

Amber finds the stairs exciting, and the minute the door is opened she is ready to explore the mysterious upstairs.

*T*he great fireplace is the heart of the house, as it has always been. When the children were small, the black iron kettle hung from the crane most of the time, with soup simmering or a pot roast sending out savory odors. The milking stool on the hearth is comfortable to sit on while stirring whatever is cooking.

The fireplace bench is an early church bench and could not have been easy to sit on but is fine for holding the teacups or coffee mugs.

The clock has an interesting history, for it was my mother's—and perhaps her mother's—and traveled all over the country with her when Father was a mining engineer. Now it stands on the mantle, and if I look inside I can read the faded announcement that it was made in Waterbury. It takes sixteen to twenty minutes to go to Waterbury from Stillmeadow. So, in a way, the clock has come home.

The milk-glass apothecary jars were full of dead beetles when we found them in an old barn but presumably had once held medicines. The lettering is ebony and the decoration dark gold.

*T*ommy Phillips has been Stillmeadow's favorite redhead since he was ten years old. Now, at sixteen, he has to stoop to get through the doorways. He lives around the corner on Jeremy Swamp Road, near enough to drop in almost daily. He was my maintenance man until he went to school in Danbury the past year and arranged for Erwin to take over.

Now often on weekends both boys swing down the road to fill the house with laughter. I find boys have the same exuberance for life that puppies have and manage about the same amount of jumping and tumbling. I am happiest when one or two are underfoot.

$\mathcal{E}$rwin is my neighbor who comes after school every day, bringing the mail up the hill. At fourteen, he is a slight quiet boy with grey-blue eyes and sunny hair—about as far from the teen-agers in the news as can be imagined.

After he has his hot cocoa, he builds a fire on the great hearth, fills the bird-feeders and burns the trash. Then we usually drive to the village to do the errands, having a comfortable visit meanwhile.

Wednesday he goes to Danbury for his violin lesson and weekly practice as second violin in the orchestra and Wednesday seems lonely at the farm, so that I am happy to see Thursday come along, bringing my boy back.

$\mathcal{E}$rwin is a valiant shoveler, and there is always plenty of shoveling at Stillmeadow in winter. Sometimes the drifts top the picket fence, and Erwin slides over the top and battles his way to the snow shovel. The path to the back door is the one we keep open because the approach is level.

This winter we used all the Cape Cod sand my son-in-law was saving for a sandy beach at the pond, plus enough rock salt to kill the lawn, but there were a few days when Erwin barely managed to reach the house and advised against my trying to get out. "I fell down three times," he said.

The grandchildren are enchanted with the white clean snow when they come out weekends from New York. They roll in it, burrow in it, nibble it. Snow is happiness for children. I notice that even as he shovels, Erwin sings softly to himself.

Cleaning the snow from the pond in December is a project involving neighbor children as well as the family. It begins when Daddy tests the pond, on the theory that if the ice is not solid, he should be the one to plunge into nine feet of icy water, and never mind how he would get out.

Then shovels and scoops come from the woodshed, and everyone takes turns at what is at best a temporary solution, for it will always snow 2 or 3 inches that night.

I do not know how much snow is supposed to weigh, but I think it is heavier than cement. It takes a good deal of hot chocolate with marshmallows to revive a pond-clearing crew.

This is the front room from the opposite side, showing bookshelves and the brass samovar, which stays on the wide windowsill, partly because we never have discovered how to use it but admire its shape and shine. The straight pine chair by the front door is my favorite of all the early chairs, with pegged construction and delicately shaped top.

From the windows the land slopes to a wildflower meadow and then the swamp, which has a beauty at any season but in spring is a whole color spectrum.

The cupboard in the front room is *not* full of books! My dark red wax unicorn figurines needed a special sanctuary. They would break so easily, and I often think they might melt if they were to get too hot. The wax must have been poured into a mold, for the unicorns are identical even to the delicate swirls on the horns. Despite the fact that my real unicorn is the color of moonlight and I see him when the violets bloom, the deep cherry color of the little wax figures is satisfying and seems to glow like rubies.

The emerald-green goblets sing a sweet crystalline note if you tap them with a fingernail, and when you hold them up to the light, they glitter.

The small upstairs corner bedroom is gay with old-fashioned faded cherry wallpaper and mellow pine furniture. The quilt is white with navy appliqué patterns and very fine quilting. It belonged to my grandmother.

Her room always smelled of sweet lavender, and whenever I walk past the quilt I seem to catch a faint fragrance of lavender in the room.

The maple spool bed has the holes in the framework where the ropes once went to support the feather mattresses.

From this window in May you look out on an apple tree in bloom.

*C*onnie, my daughter, and Alice, the nine-year-old, investigate something Alice discovered at the edge of the pond. Curt and Anne and I watch from the back yard and wait for a report, which is always breathless.

Everything at Stillmeadow is exciting, from an old bird's nest in the well house to a hoot owl in the apple tree on a winter night. The back kitchen is always full of wilting wildflowers, bird feathers, colored stones. Anne's only grief was when she tried to collect icicles and on the warm kitchen counter they simply vanished. It is easy to cry when one is seven!

But I notice adults often try to save something just as transient and cry as easily!

*F*ortunately Daddy is athletic and can keep up with his agile daughters. He also enjoys the game as much as they do. It reminds me of the saying that families who play together stick together.

Alice, at nine, is learning on the side that always being the winner is not as important as playing fairly. Her naturally competitive spirit gentles as the game goes on. Anne is too busy mastering the racket to wonder who will win.

Curt, their daddy, spent a frustrating weekend building eight birdhouses according to the specifications for bluebirds. Bluebirds began to vanish as the old rail fences were replaced by aluminum or steel, for there are no cosy holes in metal. By the next weekend someone had moved into one birdhouse, and Alice and Anne investigated, much to the dismay of the tenant— a song sparrow.

But then there was no sign saying "Bluebirds Only!"

*P*utting on a sweater involves serious concentration when you are Anne's age. One sleeve goes in neatly, but the other winds itself around the back of the neck and then somehow falls to the ground. But Anne has determination and a long span of attention.

She also has a special feeling for words and rushes in to say, "Mommy, there is an argument of ducks down on the pond!"

There is always a noise when the ducklings skim across the water in early spring. The songbirds sing at nesting time, and the music of the peepers adds to the chorus.

$\mathcal{T}$he farmhouse across the road has been empty a good many years because of legal complications when an estate was settled. Birds nest in it, rats scurry through holes in the foundations, squirrels scamper under the roof. Originally it was a charming house with the central chimney, the borning room at the right of the keeping room, and a small corner fireplace in the front room such as is rarely seen. I used to go over and visit the dear farm wife who lived there with her family when we first came to Stillmeadow.

There was no heat except for the fireplaces and the kitchen range, and there was no electricity or plumbing. But my friend was always cheerful and smiling as she lugged water from the flowing spring by the barn or came in from the woods with gunnysacks of wild mushrooms.

*T*he old milk room makes a fine kitchen, with mellow pine-paneled cupboards, electricity, and running water. In early days pails were lowered into the well and hauled up by cranking a big wheel. The wheel and pulley are still hanging in the well, and I often wonder how many buckets were lugged into the milk room during a day.

The cast-iron sink was under the window but had, of course, no faucets.

But, oh, how good the fresh milk smelled when it came in warm and creamy from the barn! Most milk today smells of wax containers, but I have been in Oscar Lovdal's milk room when his modern steel tank was full, and I know that when the top is lifted a fragrance sweeter than any honey comes from the rich moon-white milk. Smells are almost impossible to describe, but this evokes the essence of summer, sweet clover, sun-warmed hay, ripening blackberries.

A special feature of this Stillmeadow kitchen is that, though it is narrow, it spans the width of the house, so sun is always coming in. I suppose it might be called a Pullman kitchen, and it is my favorite size, for it is one step from refrigerator to counter to stove.

*T*he breakfast bar in the kitchen is also a supper bar and a lunchtime bar for the grandchildren and a sandwich bar for unexpected visitors. The window looks across the yard to the front picket fence and is framed with part of the collection of old plates.

It makes a fine place, too, for Amber's tray, for an Abyssinian does not like to eat on the floor—few cats do. Her tray goes at the right so she can eat and watch for Erwin at the same time.

The small pine cupboard at the far right is an item no kitchen should be without. It is especially for cookbooks. An assortment of cookbooks is a homemaker's constant friend, but doesn't help if looking for some special recipe involves hunting all over the house for the book.

Connie has lunch ready on the terrace by the pool. Alice and Anne are too busy to be hungry, and my-son-in-law, Curt, is off with Don Bender, our good friend, hiking around the farm.

The summerhouse has had its spring cleaning by Erwin, and the sea chest and lawn furniture are back. I wonder what the Indian encampment looked like in the days when the Indians were living by the stream? And what kind of cabin first stood on the ancient stone foundation which now supports our summerhouse? Hand-hewn logs, one room, a fireplace I think, for heating and cooking.

But the stream was stuffed with trout just asking to be cooked over the embers, and Indian corn was ripe to be roasted, and in season wild turkeys winged over.

$\mathcal{D}$on and Curt and Connie sit in the dreamy warmth of the spring sun having lunch by the pond. Alice and Anne have gulped their sandwiches and are already back in the small boat.

One special enchantment of lunch by the pond is the quietness. The only sound is the occasional clucking of chickens up the hill, the delicate music of the song sparrows and the friendly barking of the neighbor's collies. The ear-destroying sound of city traffic, the scream of sirens, and roar of subways belong to another world. I notice some city guests arrive sounding as loud as trumpeter swans, but in an hour or so their voices are lowered to a natural pitch. People begin to move slower, too, as they subconsciously realize they do not have to dodge taxis and fight to get somewhere on time.

The magic world of childhood has a breathless atmosphere. Alice at nine and Anne at seven cruise on the pond, which is not a pond at all but a mysterious sea full of sunken treasures and mermaids and dolphins. The fact that it is full of muskrats and minnows has nothing to do with it. The brown trout Daddy stocked it with may jump up any minute—and might jump right in the boat!

The water flows in near the big granite boulder, and when the pond is full, it boils down the outlet, pours through a culvert and joins George's brook on the other side of the road. In early spring during the snow melt, it is a river, but by August it is a quietly wandering brook again.

$\mathcal{H}$ildegarde was born in the borning room at the farm, quite properly. Her mother, Sweet Clover, was overwhelmed when the whelping box began to fill with squeaking bundles of fur. She wore her tongue out polishing them as they bumped blindly around. Cockers are born blind, with noses the size of a big thimble. The raspberry-pink paws wave helplessly in air. In a few days the eyes open, usually one at a time, showing milky-blue pupils.

In this picture, Hildegarde's eyes still are faintly blue but were a deep onyx by the next week. Her favorite sport was wading in the pablum dish when we started supplementary feeding.

The hunting-scene wallpaper suggests a good background for one of the best of the hunting breeds, the cocker spaniel. However, all Hildegarde hunted were balls and slippers and occasional moles. Cockers are retrievers, not killers, and we never hunt.

Hildegarde was gay and loving and beautiful with the black satin and snow of her markings.

Jill

Kon-tiki and Especially Me (reading left to right) really enjoyed their obedience training except for the Long Sit and Long Down. They did not like to sit quietly while we walked away for as long as three whole minutes!

Tiki was the lone offspring of Stillmeadow Heritage, called Little Sister by everyone. I felt he was a lone raft on a big sea just as the famous Kon-Tiki. When he was a small puppy he used to ride around in my apron pocket. He was always smiling.

Especially Me, nicknamed Teddy, was one of a litter of eight born to Stillmeadow Dark Honey. We had to manage supplementary feeding, since eight is a large number of pups for a cocker. Teddy won distinction because he would not accept the nursing bottle until we turned him upside down flat on his back with four gold paws waving in the air. Then he emptied the bottle.

Stillmeadow Dark Honey had a famous father, Champion Tokalon Cream Pie, and she never forgot it! The minute Jill got out the camera, Honey began to pose serenely. She was the color of new-minted gold, and on a dreary day her coat seemed to give out light. Her eyes were seal-dark.

The one thing she could not stand was a closed door between herself and me. So she spent much of her time on the loveseat by my desk, leaning her muzzle on the edge of the desk and wagging her tail madly when I stopped to visit her.

She was a big girl, and when she had eight puppies, it was difficult for her not to squash one. Paw by careful paw she maneuvered around them until she could curl up with all the squirming eight safely encircled against her warm fur.

Jill

Stillmeadow Hollyberry Red at three months seldom sat still long enough for a photograph. The Irish is ebullient as a puppy and a roamer when grown. Holly greeted life as a daily adventure, as indeed it was! From six weeks on, she managed the house—or at least it revolved around her. The most frequent remark was, "Where's Holly?"

She might be digging a hole in the newly sodded lawn or getting stuck under the barn, or the woodshed door had slammed on her when she popped in to look for a mouse. She pounced on her first skunk. If we went to the beach she found the deadest fish in the whole area.

But when school came along, she was the fastest learner I ever trained and managed to sit-stay and do all the exercises and win her CDX—Companion Dog Excellence. She passed the tracking test leaping along on three legs, the fourth being tangled in the lead.

She was a charming hostess unless visitors stayed too late, in which case she sighed heavily, moved to the front door, and sighed again. If nobody got up, she came to the center of the group and sighed louder and led the way again to the door. This worked!

Jill

*H*olly's favorite spot was always the small sofa by the great fireplace. In muddy weather an India print covered the upholstery, and also was becoming to her deep mahogany coat. The print washed easily and never needed ironing.

When friends dropped in, Holly might be outdoors following rabbits around. In that case, her end of the sofa was used for a human. But as soon as she came in the house, the guest would jump up and say, "I'm sorry, Holly," and move to the extreme opposite end of the sofa.

Now and then a stranger might come in and sit casually on Holly's throne. Suddenly a beautiful autumn-red muzzle would be laid gently and mournfully on the invader's lap and a pair of wistful eyes look steadily up while one paw pressed on the knee. I never saw anyone, even non-dog lovers, fail to get the message and move to another seat.

To anyone who might say dogs should never be allowed on the furniture, I would point out that the furniture is more comfortable than the floor! Of course there are some misguided souls who do not think an Abyssinian kitten should sit on the typewriter keys when you are trying to finish a book.

Jill

$\mathcal{J}$udy Lovdal lives on a farm down the road a way and often drops in to help Alice and Anne with various projects. She also is the answer to those people who feel teen-agers are a menace to society.

She is gifted, artistic and musical, an honor student, a fine cook and also full of fun. The fact that she is beautiful has not bothered her at all. She has the glowing Scandinavian color, and Connie and I privately think she looks remarkably like Greta Garbo, with her high cheekbones, wide mobile mouth, candid eyes.

Her father is a full-time farmer, and her mother helps with the haying in season but always finds time to refinish antiques, listen to opera and cook gourmet meals. Both parents are lovely to look at and an inspiration to be with.

Judy is here standing by the old well house in early April before the wisteria sends out her delicate tendrils of silvery green.

*I*n 1690 there was nothing in the yard like this play contraption. Children began to work at farm chores almost as soon as they could carry a bucket. But Alice and Anne have a fine time with this swing and slide, especially when Judy Lovdal is around to do some pushing.

Anne, being two years younger, is always bringing up the rear, grimly trying to run as fast as her sister. But Alice could have a career as a marathon runner if she were masculine, so Anne never quite makes it.

One wall of the keeping room is occupied by a soft-pine blanket chest or what in later days was called a commode. The top lifts to permit bedding to fit in and now houses all of the extra table linen. The lower part stored pitcher, washbowl and slop jar. These were usually beautiful, with intricate patterns of flowers and leaves in blues, greens, lilacs and rose. One of the handsomest lamps I know was made of a slop jar.

The Hitchcock chair was my mother's and is one piece of furniture cats and dogs and children are not supposed to push around.

The unicorn is a copy of part of the unicorn tapestry in the Cloisters in New York City. The unicorn is my favorite legendary figure, and my personal unicorn comes to the pond on moonlit May nights, cropping the wild white violets as he moves.

$\mathcal{O}$ur front door at Christmastime wears a gorgeous Della Robbia wreath which was a gift from two artistic friends. The whole snow-deep yard seems to catch the glowing colors in this wreath. When it comes down, Erwin and I spend a full hour packing it tenderly in tissue, then tucking it in a big carton. Erwin seals the cartons and vanishes to an upstairs closet. We do not trust the attic in case the squirrels come in; they might eat the nuts, varnish and all.

The storm door, alas, is a concession to the below-zero weather we get in January. Behind it, the regular door is a Dutch door—the upper half can be opened by itself, so that is where I stand on cold days to wave good-by to the children, as they leave after the weekend. Dutch doors are so convenient that I wonder more modern builders don't use them.